VISION BOARD
CLIP ART
FOR TEENS

An Empowering Magazine Book of 450+ Images, Words, Phrases, Affirmations, Vision Board Supplies & More for Teen Boys & Girls to Visualize, Manifest & Collage Life Goals & Dreams

DISCOVER YOUR TRUE SELF & UNLOCK YOUR POTENTIAL

Welcome to your complete guide to unlocking your full potential. Inside these pages, you'll find a treasure trove of inspiration, advice, and creative tools to help you navigate the journey of self-discovery and empowerment.

Are you ready to begin a journey of self-discovery, growth, and making your dreams come true? This book isn't just about flipping through pretty pages; it's about diving deep into the realms of possibility, using affirmations, imagery, and the tools to shape your future.

With over 100 pages filled with vivid imagery, motivational quotes, and practical exercises, each section is carefully designed to address key areas of your life:

   (a) Growth/Self-Improvement: From boosting confidence to overcoming challenges and fostering a positive mindset, these pages are your companion on the journey of personal growth.
   (b) Graduation/Future Planning: As you stand at the edge of adulthood, we'll help you map out your path with sections dedicated to college goals, career exploration, and imagining life beyond high school.
   (c) Health/Fitness: Your well-being is extremely important, so we've included content to inspire workout motivation, develop healthy habits, and celebrate body positivity.
   (d) Creativity/Artistic Expression: Free your inner artist with prompts to explore new hobbies, develop talents, and experiment with photography and design.
   (e) Manifestation/Law of Attraction: Dive into the principles of vision boarding, affirmations, and gratitude as you learn to harness the power of making your biggest dreams a reality.
   (f) Mindfulness/Self-Care: Nurture your mental health, find relief from stress, practice self-love, and master the art of work-life balance.

But that's not all. We've left space for you to personalize your journey with blank pages, inviting you to articulate your own goals and dreams.

This book is your roadmap to empowerment. It's time to visualize, make your dreams reality, and create a collage of the life you want. Let's begin this adventure together!

PREPARING YOUR MINDSET

Before jumping into all the colorful activities in this book, let's get our mindset ready for the awesome journey ahead.

1. Keep an Open Mind:

Approach this book with an open mind, believing that you have the power to create the future you want.

2. Be Ready to Learn:

Be willing to let go of any negative thoughts or limits you've put on yourself. This is about seeing your true potential.

3. Use Your Imagination:

Your thoughts and visualizations can actually shape your reality in powerful ways. Pretty cool, right?

4. Stay Curious:

Approach each activity with an eager, curious mindset, ready to learn new things about yourself.

5. Discover Your Dreams:

This book will help you discover your true passions and biggest dreams. Listen to your heart and intuition.

With your mind open and ready, let's dive in and start creating the life you really want to live!

CREATING A VISION BOARD: A STEP-BY-STEP GUIDE

To get the most out of this book, follow these steps:

1. Get Your Goal On: Figure out what you want to achieve and let that drive you forward.

2. Check It Out: Explore the different sections and themes to see what cool stuff is inside.

3. Pick Your Path: Choose the areas that speak to you the most, or mix and match different sections that catch your eye.

4. Dive In: Read the inspiring quotes, think about the prompts, and soak up all the wisdom.

5. Dream Big: Use the clipart, images, and affirmations to bring your dreams and goals to life.

6. Reflect and Write: Take time to think about what you've experienced, learned, and realized, and write about your journey.

7. Make It Happen: Turn your dreams into reality by taking steps towards your goals.

8. Rinse and Repeat: Come back to the book whenever you need inspiration, guidance, or a fresh perspective. Feel free to revisit sections as many times as you want.

9. Share Your Story: Share your experiences and creations with others, and inspire them to start their own empowerment journey.

10. Celebrate Yourself: Give yourself props for your achievements, no matter how big or small. Recognize how far you've come and how much you've grown.

By following these steps and embracing the journey, this book will be your go-to guide for self-discovery, empowerment, and making your dreams a reality. So, dive in and let the magic happen.

Your dreams are worth visualizing – let this clipart book be your ticket to success.

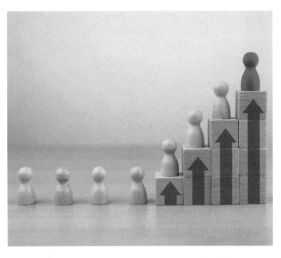

THE FUTURE
DEPENDS
ON WHAT YOU
DO TODAY

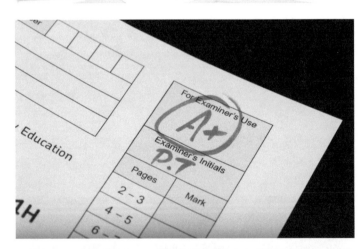

ONE SMALL
POSITIVE THOUGHT
IN THE MORNING
CAN CHANGE YOUR
WHOLE DAY

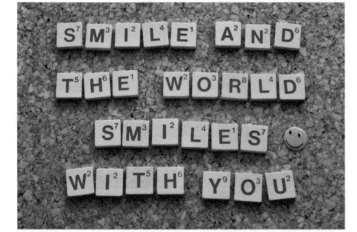

SMILE AND
THE WORLD
SMILES
WITH YOU

Today is
gonna be a
good day
♥♥♥

I ♥
ME

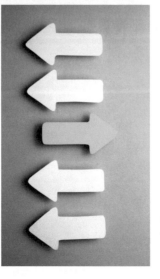

Turn
your
weaknesses
into
strengths

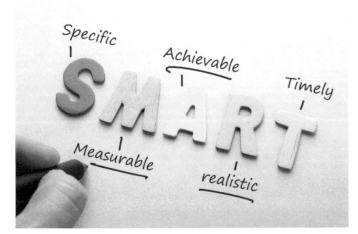

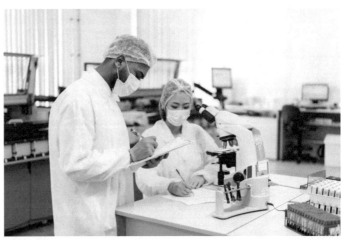

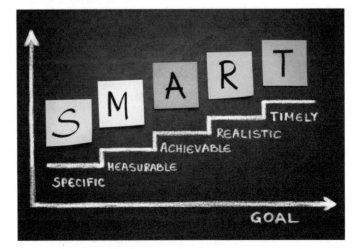

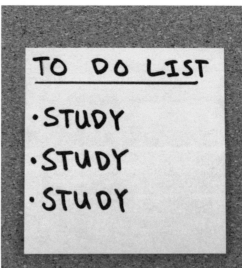

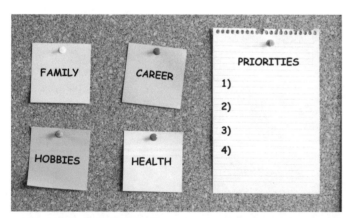

PERSONAL
LOANS
TO FIT
YOUR
BUDGET

Pay
As
You
Earn

Live a purposeful
and abundant life.

Specific
measurable
Achievable
Realistic
Timely

COLLEGE

SET GOAL

MAKE PLAN

GET TO WORK

STICK TO iT

REACH GOAL

BE THE
GAME
CHANGER

Your body is not a problem to be solved

LOVE YOUR BODY

ALL BODIES ARE BEAUTIFUL

Love your body Because you only have one

GRATITUDE IS THE BEST ATTITUDE !

Gratitude turns what we have into enough

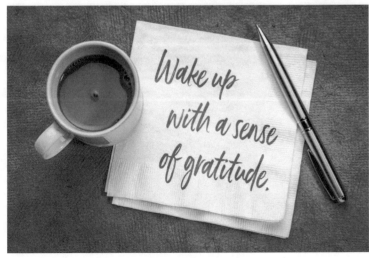

Wake up with a sense of gratitude.

EXPRESS YOUR GRATITUDE

MENTAL
HEALTH
MATTERS

YOU ARE
DOING BETTER
THAN YOU
THINK YOU ARE

you are
not
alone

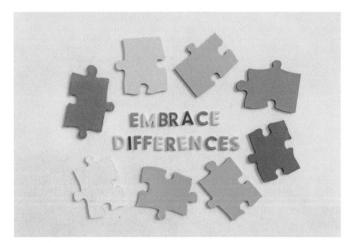

EMBRACE
DIFFERENCES

BE KIND TO
YOURSELF

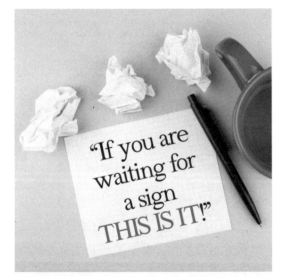

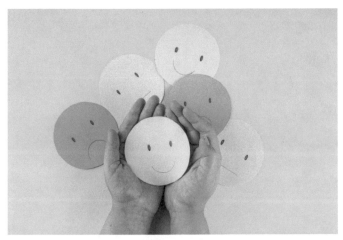

NOTICE
YOUR
SENSES

YOU ARE
NOT
ALONE

DECIDE
COMMIT
FOCUS
SUCCEED

LIFE IS A BEAUTIFUL ADVENTURE

a a a a b b b b c c c c d d d d e e
e e f f f f g g g g h h h h i i i i j j
j j k k k k l l l l m m m m n n n n o
o o o p p p p q q q q r r r r s s s s
t t t t u u u u v v v v w w w w x
x x x y y y y z z z z , , , , ... / /
/ / ¡ ¡ ¡ ¡ ' ' ' ' : : : : » » » » ! ! ! !
% % % % ^ ^ ^ ^ &
& & & * * (( )) — + + = =

You're DOING Great

ALL GOOD >THINGS<

THE BEST VERSION OF YOURSELF

STAY Humble Hustle HARD

be you; do you; for you!

THINK like THERE IS NO BOX

YOUR ONLY LIMIT IS your MIND

EVERY journey NEEDS A first STEP

I love MYSELF TO THE moon AND BACK

LIFE IS TOO SHORT TO SPEND it at war WITH YOURSELF

DONT LET your SIZE HINDER YOUR style WEAR WHAT YOU WANT

WHEN THINGS change INSIDE YOU things CHANGE AROUND YOU

FIND GRATITUDE IN ALL THE mome nts

Always BELIEVE IN impos sible

DONT STAND IN your OWN WAY

all bodies are good bodies

BODY positive

GOALS

Fitness

TIME to STUDY

GOOD TIMES GOOD VIBES

DRINK ME !!!

WORK OUT

WISH LIST

TRiP

chill
out

THANK YOU
♥

WELL
DONE

GOOD
JOB

self
care

grateful
thankful
blessed

good
vibes

wow

VISION BOARD

VACATION

inspire

Believe

Manifest

SUCCESS

Grateful!

Hope

Calm

together

relax

Happy

FEARLESS

STRENGTH

Purpose

memories

WARM UP ✓ DONE

TO DO Notes

EXAM POSITIVE mind Math

SPORT SUMMER

beautiful Peacful

QUIZ Science GRADES

2025 VISION BOARD

Happy New Year 2025

New Year's Resolutions
√ Improve self
√ Save money
√ Get fit
√ Eat Better
√ Find better job
√ More family time
√ Help others
√ More travel
√ Enjoy life!

HAPPY NEW YEAR

2025
say yes
to new adventures

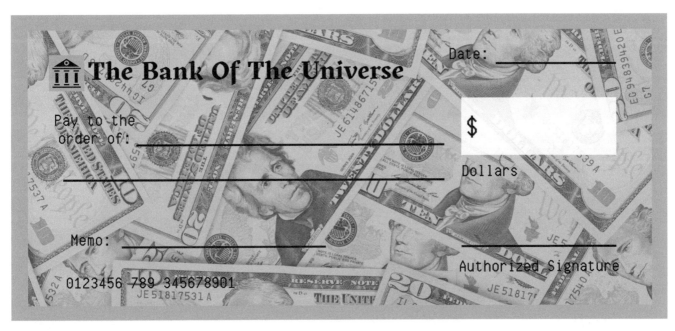

THANK YOU!

Thank you for breathing life into your aspirations with these inspiring clipart images and your boundless creativity! We appreciate you taking the time to embrace the empowering journey of visualizing your dreams through the pages of this book. May the focused energy you've invested in crafting your vision boards continue to fuel your passion and drive you towards achieving your goals.

If you're feeling motivated, scan the QR code to share how assembling these vibrant vision boards has opened your mind or ignited a fire within you. Your uplifting story about the transformative experience of bringing your dreams to life through visuals could provide hope and encouragement to others seeking to embark on their own journey of self-discovery and manifestation.

Made in United States
Cleveland, OH
28 December 2024

12744402R20061